BOOK ANALYSIS

Written by Nathalie Roland
and Claire Mathot
Translated by Soline de Dorlodot
and Rebecca Neal

The Name of the Rose

by Umberto Eco

Bright
≡Summaries.com

BOOK ANALYSIS

Shed new light
on your favorite books with

Bright
≡Summaries.com

www.brightsummaries.com

UMBERTO ECO — 9

THE NAME OF THE ROSE — 13

SUMMARY — 15

- A strange death
- The investigation begins
- A second murder
- A lethal poison
- A book and its secrets
- The mysteries of the library
- Solving the mystery

CHARACTER STUDY — 25

- The people from the world beyond the abbey
- The characters from the abbey
- The victims

ANALYSIS — 37

- A hybrid novel
- The role of religion
- Intertextuality
- A labyrinthine novel

FURTHER REFLECTION — 55

FURTHER READING — 59

UMBERTO ECO

ITALIAN NOVELIST AND ESSAYIST

- **Born in Alessandria (Italy) in 1932.**
- **Died in Milan in 2016.**
- **Notable works:**
  - *Foucault's Pendulum* (1988), novel
  - *The Island of the Day Before* (1994), novel
  - *History of Beauty* (2004), essay

The Italian author Umberto Eco was a prolific novel and essay writer, and his work has garnered recognition and acclaim around the world. He was a linguist by training and specialised in semiotics (the study of signs and their meanings), philosophy and literature.

His novels, which include *The Name of the Rose* and *Foucault's Pendulum*, skilfully combine detective intrigue and literary and historical references. He also published more philosophical works, such as *History of Beauty* and *On Ugliness* (2007), in which he illustrates how the concepts of beauty and ugliness have evolved throughout history by analysing sculptures, paintings and literary works dating from antiquity through to the present day.

THE NAME OF THE ROSE

A MEDIEVAL DETECTIVE STORY

- **Genre:** novel
- **Reference edition:** Eco, U. (2004) *The Name of the Rose*. London: Vintage.
- **1st edition:** 1980
- **Themes:** murder, investigation, labyrinth, library, history of the Middle Ages, religion, poison

The Name of the Rose was Umberto Eco's first novel.

It is set in the early 14th century and follows the characters of William of Baskerville and his scribe Adso of Melk as they travel to Italy during a time of religious discord. While they are staying in an abbey, a string of murders shatters the community's peace. William and Adso try to solve these crimes, as well as the many mysteries surrounding the abbey's library. Their investigation draws them into the abbey's labyrinthine library, where they search for a mysterious book.

SUMMARY

Eco claims that *The Name of the Rose* is based on a manuscript containing the memoirs of Adso of Melk, a young Benedictine monk (the Benedictines are a religious order that ascribe great importance to intellectual and physical work, including the copying of manuscripts). As a young man, Adso was sent to Italy, where he became the scribe and disciple of William of Baskerville, a Franciscan monk (a religious order whose members are bound by a vow of poverty). Together, Adso and William experience a series of unusual events in an abbey in northern Italy in late 1327.

A STRANGE DEATH

William and Adso arrive at a wealthy Benedictine abbey located on a mountain. They are welcomed by the abbot, and explain the reason for their visit to him: William has been sent to meet the Benedictine superiors in order to find out which of them support the emperor. The abbot suspects Remigio of having been a member of a heretical sect (meaning a sect that has been condemned by the Church because its beliefs are seen as contrary to the true faith), and voices staunch opposition to these sects: "Kill them all; God will recognize His own" (p. 145). He also asks William and Adso to investigate Adelmo's death: he fell from one of the towers of the library one stormy night, but it remains unclear whether this was suicide or murder.

The abbot gives William free rein to investigate: he is granted permission to question the other monks and investigate everywhere in the abbey apart from the library, even though this is the place where the crime took place and, as William soon realises, the key to understanding the events. Only a select few are permitted to enter the library, which "defends itself" (p. 30); if the rumours are to be believed, it is protected by magic. However, although access to the library is strictly regulated, the floor where it is located is often lit up at night.

THE INVESTIGATION BEGINS

William and Adso begin their investigation by meeting Ubertino of Casale (Italian Franciscan,

1259-1329), with whom they discuss the divisions that have arisen within the Benedictine order because of extremist movements. They then question Severinus, the herbalist, to find out whether Adelmo's fall could have been caused by hallucinations after ingesting certain herbs.

Next, they go to the scriptorium, where the monks copy manuscripts, and are greeted by Malachi, the librarian. William gathers information about Aldemo's illustrations. When laughter breaks out, the offending monks are severely reprimanded by Jorge, an elderly blind monk, and a debate about the role of laughter ensues. Afterwards, the two investigators go to the forge, where they question Nicholas, the master glazier of the abbey.

A SECOND MURDER

The next day, during the first prayers, frightened servants burst into the church and inform the monks that they have found Venantius's body in a basin filled with pig's blood. The two investigators find out that both Adelmo and Venantius had made a request of Berengar, the assistant librarian, and they meet Alinardo, who tells them that it is possible to get into the library through the ossarium. By observing the library from the outside, William manages to deduce its layout.

Later on, Benno tells William and Adso that Berengar was in love with Adelmo and that Adelmo would have done anything to get his hands on a particular book that he had spent many years looking for. That night, the two investigators sneak into the scriptorium, and William notices an interesting parchment with a coded message lying on Venantius's table. They are interrupted by a mysterious nocturnal visitor (Berengar), who steals two books and William's glasses.

They then enter the library, which is utterly labyrinthine. A verse from the Apocalypse (the final book in the Bible, more commonly known as the Book of Revelation) is written over the entrance to each room. They soon realise that the library's layout is based on geography, with areas for England, Spain, Africa, and so on, but they do not manage to get into the secret *finis Africae* room.

A LETHAL POISON

In the morning, they hear that Berengar has disappeared, and shortly afterwards they discover his body in the baths. When William and Severinus examine the body, they see that the tips of Berengar's fingers are brown, like those of the previous victim. Severinus knows which poison is behind this phenomenon: it disappeared from his laboratory after the storm.

Adso meets Salvatore and questions him about a heretic, Fra Dolcino. William takes this opportunity to explain to Adso that heretics have their good and bad sides just like everybody else, and that the Pope's primary motivation for denouncing them is that they represent a political threat to him. However, this does not satisfy Adso's curiosity about heresy, and when he asks Ubertino for explanations about Fra Dolcino, he finds out that the latter criticised the Church and inspired a popular revolt that was brutally repressed. William and Adso then question Remigio, a former disciple of Dolcino.

A BOOK AND ITS SECRETS

In the kitchen, a young woman seduces Adso, and they spend the night together. William chides his friend after he tells him about his nocturnal exploits, but makes allowances because he knows that the girl was a poor peasant who was prostituting herself to feed her family. While discussing the progress of the investigation, they realise that the murders correspond to the excerpts from the Apocalypse. Moreover, William has fully decoded the message left by Venantius and now knows that the murderer is trying to prevent certain secrets, which are contained within a book, from coming to light.

A Franciscan delegation arrives at the abbey. They believe that Pope John XXII's (1245-1334) actions are not befitting of his role, as he is constantly amassing wealth and has decided to impose a tax on sinners. A delegation from Avignon then arrives, led by the Dominican Bernard Gui.

The two groups meet to discuss Christ's poverty, his status and the religious orders' attitude towards heretics. Bernard Gui arrests Salvatore and a woman accused of being a witch.

THE MYSTERIES OF THE LIBRARY

Meanwhile, Severinus realises that Berengar must have gone to the hospital before going to the baths, because he finds the book that the assistant librarian had stolen from the scriptorium in his laboratory. However, Severinus's body is then found in the laboratory, but the book is nowhere to be seen. Suspicion immediately falls on Remigio, who is arrested. His trial is conducted by Bernard Gui, who is convinced that he is guilty and brutally interrogates him.

William suspects Benno of being the thief, as he knows that he is prepared to do anything to discover the secrets contained in the library's books. However, Benno has just been appointed assistant librarian: now that he has ties to the library, he cannot discuss the manuscripts.

Nicholas, the master glazier, tells William and Adso that the appointment of every new assistant librarian has been met with criticism. On his way back to the scriptorium, William begins to wonder whether the murders could be motivated by the fierce competition for the post. He warns the abbot that his life is in danger, as he knows the secrets of the library.

The next day, during the morning prayers, Malachi staggers into the church before collapsing. William notices that his tongue is black, which is a sign that he has been poisoned, and realises that all the victims knew Greek.

SOLVING THE MYSTERY

William and Adso go to the library at night and realise that someone is inside. They finally manage to get into the secret room, where they find Jorge. The blind monk has poisoned a book containing several works (including Aristotle's [Greek philosopher, 384-322 BCE] *Poetics* [c. 335 BCE]) which discuss the importance of divine laughter, in order to prevent anyone from revealing this information.

It transpires that all the victims died because they came into contact with this book, apart from Adelmo, who committed suicide after hearing of its contents before Jorge poisoned the manuscript. The poison killed the people who touched the pages of the book, namely Venantius, Berengar and Malachi. Severinus was killed by Malachi, who was in love with Berengar and thought that the latter had been unfaithful to him with Adelmo and Severinus.

After telling them everything, Jorge commits suicide by eating the poisoned pages of the book. William and Adso try to save the manuscript, but a lamp falls and sets the library and the whole abbey on fire.

William and Adso leave the abbey and go their separate ways. Years later, Adso returns and collects all the pages he can.

CHARACTER STUDY

THE PEOPLE FROM THE WORLD BEYOND THE ABBEY

Adso of Melk

Adso of Melk, the story's narrator, is an elderly Benedictine monk in the monastery of Melk in Austria. As he approaches the end of his life, he writes a manuscript in Latin in which he recounts one of his formative experiences, a seven-day adventure in an abbey in northern Italy. His aim is to leave an account of this adventure for future generations, without passing judgement on it. Eco claims that this manuscript was subsequently translated into a number of different languages by a variety of writers, and that he has taken it upon himself to translate it into Italian in the 20th century.

In 1327, when he was a novice in the monastery of Melk, Adso's father took him to Italy, where he met William of Baskerville and became his scribe and disciple. In spite of his youth, Adso tries to understand the turmoil of the period, and takes the wise and insightful William as his role model as he develops his critical thinking skills. He is obedient, insatiably curious and always eager to know more, and follows William everywhere while peppering him with questions. His youth means that he is highly impressionable, and he is fascinated by the fervour of some of the monks, which has driven them to murder and heresy, and by mysticism, as practiced by Ubertino.

Adso learns a great deal from his experience in the abbey: he discovers the passions that govern humanity, namely love, hate and the destructive power of pride, and gains a greater understanding of the religious and political issues of his time, including the conflicts between popes and secular leaders, the various forms of heresy, and the Inquisition (a judicial institution of the Catholic Church which was established to combat heresy).

William of Baskerville

William of Baskerville is a learned Franciscan monk, and Adso of Melk has been placed under his tutelage, making him something of a father figure to the young novice. He is around 50 years old and is described as tall and very thin, with a lively gaze. In spite of his occasional spells of apathy, he is generally a very energetic man.

He previously served as an inquisitor in France and England, but he has left this role and come to the abbey to meet a delegation of Franciscans and take part in a theological debate on Christ's poverty. The delegation's purpose is to agree on their order's position with regard to the new pope in Avignon. This is a highly sensitive issue, as it risks provoking a schism within the Church.

William is known among the monks for his intelligence, shrewdness and curiosity. The abbot Abo asks him to solve the mystery of Adelmo's murder, and to make his task easier he gives him permission to talk to everyone and roam freely through the abbey. His approach to the mystery is very rational, and he takes inspiration from one of his friends, the English philosopher and theologian William of Ockham (1285-1349), who believes that any problem can be solved using logic. One of his main aims in taking on the investigation is to solve the case rationally and, in doing so, to show the other monks that there is no reason to assume that the Devil is behind everything, although he is also motivated by a sense of intellectual pride.

Eco drew inspiration for the character of William from two figures, one real and one fictional. These are Sherlock Holmes (the main character of the novels of Arthur Conan Doyle [1859-1930]) and William of Ockham respectively, which clearly illustrates the value he placed on rational, logical thinking

Bernard Gui (also known as Bernardo Guidoni)

This character is a historical figure who really existed. He was a Dominican monk and inquisitor, and in the novel he is in charge of restoring order in the monastery. He is hypocritical, sarcastic and domineering, and when he conducts Remigio's trial, he is so convinced of his guilt that he has no qualms about fabricating evidence against him. He is a frightening character who likes to flaunt his authority and inspire fear in others.

THE CHARACTERS FROM THE ABBEY

The abbot Abo

Abo is the head of the Franciscan abbey and asks William to solve the mystery of Adelmo's death. He is proud of the wealth acquired by the monastery and takes a hard line when it comes to heretics, even going so far as to say that they should be executed. He is overwhelmed by the events taking place in his abbey, is concerned about its reputation, and tries to maintain order and calm.

Jorge of Burgos

Jorge is the second-oldest monk in the abbey, and is blind. He is respected by the other monks, who are impressed by his age and wisdom, and he serves as confessor for many of them. He is a firm believer in the monastery's rules and refuses to countenance any failure to respect them. For example, he is staunchly opposed to laughter and idle chatter, which he believes have no place in the abbey.

He takes a particularly dim view of laughter: according to him, it is acceptable for the poor, but is wholly inappropriate for the educated elites (the monks), because if they get into the habit of laughing, they will lose their respect and fear for everything they should hold most sacred, such as God. He therefore views laughter as dangerous for monks.

We eventually learn that Jorge is responsible for the murders committed in the abbey. He spread poison on the pages of the second volume of Aristotle's *Poetics*, which takes comedy (and therefore laughter) as its subject, so that any overly curious monks would poison themselves. He is so convinced that this knowledge about laughter is dangerous that he would rather eat the pages of the book, knowing that the poison will kill him, than see their contents revealed.

Salvatore of Montferrat

Salvatore suffers from an illness and speaks an imaginary language made up of all the languages he knows. After surviving a massacre, he wandered aimlessly, pretending to be ill or poor so that people would take pity on him, before entering the order. He is arrested by Bernard Gui for allegedly practising magic and talking to a witch. In some ways, he resembles an animal.

Ubertino of Casale

Ubertino is another character who really existed. He is described as an eccentric old man, and belongs to a movement which advocates reforming the Dominican order to ensure that it follows Christ's teachings more closely, in particular by practising poverty. He is familiar with the heretic movements, and takes a hardline stance on them.

Remigio of Varagine

This portly man is the abbey's cellarer, meaning that he is in charge of food and supplies. He previously belonged to a group of heretics led by Fra Dolcino. Although he entered the abbey voluntarily, he does not share the order's religious convictions and does not uphold his vow of chastity. He is the prime suspect in Severinus's murder.

Benno of Uppsala

According to William, Benno "has a lust for knowledge" (p. 387) and would give anything to know the secrets of the library. This drives him to steal the book from Severinus, and shortly after doing so he is appointed assistant librarian to replace Berengar, who has been murdered. As a guardian of the library, he can no longer divulge any information about the manuscripts.

THE VICTIMS

Adelmo of Otranto

This young monk, who is in charge of the illuminations (the manuscripts' illustrations), is the first to die: he falls from the library tower during a snowstorm in the middle of the night. It is unclear whether he committed suicide or was murdered.

Venantius of Salvemec

The second victim is an expert in the Greek language. The night before his death, he had argued with Jorge about laughter.

His body is found in a container full of pig's blood. He was killed because he had overheard a conversation between Adelmo and Berengar, and because he had held the book.

Berengar of Arundel

Berengar is the assistant librarian, and becomes the third murder victim. As he suffers from convulsions, he often takes warm baths to calm them. This is where he is found dead during the third night of the story. He was murdered because he stole the book, preventing William from understanding why its contents had driven Adelmo to suicide, which would have allowed him to solve the mystery more quickly.

Severinus of Sankt Wendel

As the abbey's herbalist, Severinus is in charge of the baths, the hospital and the vegetable garden. He has an excellent knowledge of poisons and helps William to examine the bodies of the victims. He discovers the book that Berengar had stolen, but is murdered by Malachi on the fifth day. He and William are the only characters to work out the book's deadly secret.

Malachi of Hildesheim

Malachi is in charge of the library and is very careful to protect its secrets. He is in love with Berengar, but when he suspects that Berengar has been unfaithful to him, he gives Bernard Gui the letters he wrote about the heretics. When Benno brings him back the book that had been stolen, his curiosity ends up getting him killed.

ANALYSIS

A HYBRID NOVEL

Genre is an important element of literary history, as classifying a novel as part of a particular movement enables us to better understand its characteristics, influences and impact. However, some novels, such as *The Name of the Rose*, defy straightforward categorisation.

The novel has the characteristics of at least three genres, namely the detective novel, the historical novel and the *Bildungsroman*, also known as the coming-of-age novel.

The Name of the Rose shares the main characteristics of the detective novel:

- The characters' quest is focused not on the future but on the past (a crime, which is usually committed before the start of the narrative). The character investigating the crime needs to correctly interpret the clues they find to figure out what happened and identify the culprit.

- The investigation is at the heart of the story, which means that some of its characters fit into clearly defined roles (the victim, the culprit, the investigator). However, many writers will also put their own spin on these three archetypes.
- The mystery will eventually be solved thanks to logical reasoning.

These characteristics can be clearly seen in Eco's novel, as William of Baskerville and Adso of Melk initially investigate a murder that was committed before the start of the narrative, but the scope of their investigation soon expands to encompass a number of other crimes. After a series of twists and turns, namely the string of murders, the discovery of clues and their deductions, they eventually unmask the murderer.

The Name of the Rose is also a historical novel, a genre which is characterised by the following features:

- the novel is set during a particular historical period, which tends to be described in a realistic manner;
- the novel often features a mixture of fictional

characters and people who really existed.

The Name of the Rose is set during the Middle Ages, in the early 14th century. The important people alluded to, including popes and emperors, and some of the other main characters, such as Bernard Gui and Ubertino of Casale, are real historical figures.

Furthermore, Eco claims that his novel has been adapted from an authentic medieval manuscript and describes the period's religious and political conflicts with the greatest possible realism. On the other hand, it appears that the two main characters are imaginary, having being invented by Eco.

Finally, *The Name of the Rose* has many of the features of the *Bildungsroman*. This kind of novel follows a young character, often during their adolescence, as they progress towards adulthood. Their experiences during the story shape their personality, force them to become independent, teach them about the world, and allow them to become accomplished in a particular field and attain greater wisdom.

As Adso explains in the novel, when he travelled to the abbey he was a young novice. His experiences there and William of Baskerville's influence enabled him to develop his critical thinking skills, discover human passions such as love, hate, jealousy and fear, and gain a better understanding of the issues of his time, such as heresy and the Inquisition.

The Name of the Rose is therefore a complex novel in terms of both content and form: its hybridity, as it combines the genres of detective novel, historical novel and *Bildungsroman*, makes multiple readings and multiple interpretations possible.

THE ROLE OF RELIGION

In the Middle Ages, religion played a major role in the daily lives of the powerful elites and the poor alike. The 10th and 11th centuries saw monasteries return to prominence as centres of religious activity, beginning with the establishment of Cluny Abbey in France. This led to the foundation of new monasteries across Europe. During the period the novel is set in, society tended to idealise monks, believing that they were above the vanities of the world and lived only to serve

God. There were two ways to join a monastery: some young nobles were placed in monasteries as novices while they were still children and went on to become monks (this is the case for Adso of Melk), while others entered monasteries later in life, having previously been a part of regular society.

Community life was at the heart of the monastic orders, which each had their own founder and their own particular characteristics. For example, some monks carried out manual labour, while others devoted themselves to prayer and contemplation, and still others worked on copying and preserving manuscripts. Monks often travelled between different monasteries, which facilitated the spread of ideas, and their ever-increasing level of erudition made them gatekeepers of knowledge.

The first universities were also founded around this time. They taught not only religious doctrine (theology), but also other subjects such as rhetoric, Arabic philosophy, law and logic. This resulted in new generations of educated, well-read monks who had not abandoned their faith, but did not necessarily seek out a divine explanation for all phenomena. For example, William of Baskerville's first instinct is to look for a rational explanation for the murders in the abbey.

The two main religious orders in the novel are the Franciscans and the Dominicans, both of which were mendicant orders (meaning that they travelled to other towns and villages to spread God's message) that focused their efforts on preaching and conversion. However, over time significant differences between the two orders developed:

- the Franciscans believed in poverty, as preached by their founder Francis of Assisi (c. 1182-1226), and rejected the idea of personal or collective property (although they were subsequently obliged to join together in monastic communities);
- the Dominicans were permitted to amass wealth.

In the universities, disputations, meaning rhetorical exercises which took the form of verbal debates between two people or groups on a theological issue, soon became widespread. These debates sometimes became so heated that they led to discord between different religious movements, or even within the same religious order.

For example, the issue of Christ's poverty (whether or not he had material possessions) was a pressing subject for the Franciscans. Although in theory the monks had no possessions, because monasteries and their books officially belonged to the Holy See, in practice they owned everyday items because they lived in monasteries and used the objects there.

Rifts appeared within the Franciscan Order, and Pope John XXII, who is mentioned in the novel, wanted to deal with the matter by bringing the Spirituals (the name given to the most radical Franciscans) into line.

When John XXII condemned the doctrine of the absolute poverty of Christ in 1323, some Franciscans joined forces with Louis IV, Holy Roman Emperor (c. 1282-1347), a staunch opponent of papal authority. This religious crisis therefore had political consequences, and accusations of heresy abounded.

The line between "difference of opinion" and "heresy" is often a very fine one. New religious movements were constantly emerging, each with their own doctrine, philosophy and rites. Some of them also established monasteries, and they all attracted members from the ranks of the regular population, to varying degrees. This proliferation of different orders was viewed as dangerous by the Church because it fostered division rather than unity, so the papal authorities officially condemned many orders as heretical (this is the case for the Dolcinians in the novel, for example).

TURMOIL IN THE 14TH CENTURY

During the 14th century, Europe and Christianity were both in crisis: the kings and emperors derived their authority from the Pope, but sought political independence. A quarrel between the Philip IV of France (1268-1314) and Pope Boniface VIII (1235-1303) left the entire continent divided.

Philip then named a new pope, Clement V, who established his court in Avignon, while the existing pope stayed in Rome. Each of

> the two popes tried to win support from political leaders and the religious orders in order to bolster their legitimacy. This gave rise to a wide range of opinions and differing ideas, resulting in a series of fierce disputes. The Catholic Church in Rome responded by setting up the Inquisition to suppress its opponents, who were condemned as heretics.

INTERTEXTUALITY

Intertextuality can be defined as the ways in which a text is connected with one or more other texts. These connections can be concentrated within the story and the narrative (through what the characters say, the world around them, and so on), or they can be addressed directly to the reader in ways that do not affect the story, for example through allusions, jokes or explicit references.

Intertextuality can be viewed as a kind of game between the author and the reader (the reader looks for hints dropped by the author, and understanding the intertextual references proves their cultural awareness), but it can also confer new meanings on the narrative and make new interpretations of the text possible.

The Name of the Rose is packed with intertextuality: Eco was a semiotician, linguist, historian and expert in ancient languages, like his character William of Baskerville.

William is an intellectual with an insatiable, all-consuming curiosity. Besides Aristotle's *Poetics*, which plays a key role in the story, he is interested in other authors from antiquity, as well as contemporary philosophers such as Thomas Aquinas (Italian theologian, 1225-1274), Roger Bacon (English scholar and philosopher, 1200-1292) and William of Ockham. These references all serve a purpose, as they indicate that William of Baskerville is following in the footsteps of these philosophers and theologians, particularly with regard to his methodology and his logic.

Given its medieval setting, the novel also features many references to Christian texts: the monks discuss them among themselves, and verses from the Apocalypse are written at the entrance to each room in the library. These references are clearly linked to the time period and world in which the monks live (for example, the verses from the Apocalypse in the rooms of the library are related to how the library and the books within it are organised).

The most obvious intertextual element in the novel is its protagonist's name, William of Baskerville, which brings to mind the names of two men, namely the fictional character Sherlock Holmes and William of Ockham, who really existed.

- The first name "William" is a reference to the English philosopher William of Ockham, whose freethinking inspired both admiration and fear during his lifetime.
- "Baskerville" refers to the novel *The Hound of the Baskervilles* (1902), whose main character is Sherlock Holmes. Eco wanted to establish a link between his character and Holmes through their shared method of investigation: both men gather clues, favour rational solutions over supernatural explanations, and think calmly in order to arrive at a coherent solution.

This intertextuality, which is apparent to the reader but not to the novel's characters, plays a different role than the intertextuality within the narrative. A reader who is familiar with Conan Doyle's novels will quickly pick up on the link between William of Baskerville and Sherlock Holmes, and this will give them a better understanding of his actions and reflections during the investigation.

A LABYRINTHINE NOVEL

The labyrinth, which is at once a myth, a form, a figure and a symbol, is a recurring image in a range of art forms, including literature, and in numerous branches of the humanities. Because of its intricate construction, the labyrinth is difficult to navigate by design. It originated in Greek mythology, where it was home to the Minotaur and the scene of the monstrous half-man, half-bull's struggle with Theseus.

Since then, the image of the labyrinth has become a timeless, universal representation of a paradox or a feeling of being lost. It can serve as a metaphorical representation of the difficulty or impossibility of achieving a particular goal, the sense of despair that accompanies being lost somewhere, or the hope of escaping a pursuer or an antagonist.

The labyrinths in *The Name of the Rose*

This novel contains a multitude of labyrinthine figures and symbols:

- **The library:** in spatial terms, the layout of the rooms is intended to confuse the visitor, and in spiritual terms, it is home to both "the works that enlighten […] research" (p. 27) and books containing "the lies of the infidels" (p. 29). Readers must therefore be able to tell the difference between good and bad manuscripts.
- **The world:** William explains to Adso that mankind cannot understand the logic of a world created by God, and that signs are the only things that allow us to find our way.
- **The historical context of the 14th century:** Christians are at each other's throats and new schools of thought are challenging existing religious doctrine. It becomes hard to determine who is right and who is wrong in a world of ideas that are increasingly difficult to navigate.
- **The multiple plot strands:** the reader follows

several narrative threads at once (Who is the murderer? Where is the book? What secrets does the library hold?).
- **Different readings based on the different genres:** the reader may choose to focus on the detective investigation, references to academic progress in the 14th century, or the religious controversies of the era (Christ's poverty, the various heretical sects, etc.), among other elements.
- **Eco's manuscript:** the story takes the form of a *mise en abyme* (the representation of a work within another work), given that the narrative is allegedly based on a manuscript that came into Eco's possession and is itself the translation of Adso's original manuscript. This technique makes the reader question what is true and what is false in order to navigate yet another labyrinth.

The many images of the labyrinth add to the complexity of *The Name of the Rose*.

The symbol of the labyrinth

In this section, we will examine the symbolism of the first and most obvious labyrinth featured in the book, namely the library. This labyrinth contains at least three metaphors:

- Firstly, for the two main characters, it represents the difficulty of getting to the bottom of the mystery surrounding the crimes committed within the abbey. The library's labyrinthine layout makes it difficult to solve the mystery, especially as they have to crack multiple codes in different locations. This difficulty notwithstanding, William and Adso manage to identify the culprit and work out why they committed the murders.
- In addition, for William of Baskerville, the labyrinthine complexity of the library's organisation could represent the fact that knowledge is difficult (and, according to Jorge of Burgos, dangerous) to access: we can easily wander or get lost on the path to knowledge. We cannot access it easily (from the outside), but the labyrinth can also represent a prison of knowledge (when viewed from the inside) which is only accessible to a select few. Finally, William tells Adso that attaining greater understanding of the world is a chaotic process.
- The labyrinthine library is also a metaphor for

Adso's learning process, which is sometimes complicated: the events in the abbey teach him about human passions, the world in general and the place he wants to occupy within it (for example, after his first experience of love, he makes the conscious decision to renounce it). In this way, the labyrinth can represent the relative difficulty of accessing distant, sacred and sometimes dangerous things, such as death, love and God. Adso's journey across the labyrinth with William symbolises his entry into adulthood and a greater understanding of the world.

The library that William and Adso explore therefore symbolises the seemingly impenetrable mysteries surrounding them, the difficulty and potential danger of accessing knowledge, and Adso's journey towards attaining greater knowledge. The fire at the end of the novel represents the end of their quest, the impossibility of fully knowing and understanding the world, and Adso's entry into adulthood.

Since it was first published, *The Name of the Rose* has been hailed as a masterpiece, in large part because of its wide range of possible readings.

It is at once a historical novel, a detective novel and a *Bildungsroman*, and its plot is complex and tightly structured. It appeals to both laypeople, who can read it for entertainment and relaxation, and more educated readers, who will find themselves plunged into a labyrinth crammed with double meanings and intertextual references. This fusion of erudition and a fast-moving plot is undoubtedly central to the novel's enduring popularity.

FURTHER REFLECTION

SOME QUESTIONS TO THINK ABOUT...

- *The Name of the Rose* displays the characteristics of several genres. What are they? Explain your answer.
- In the novel, the monks argue about the poverty of Christ. Why does this debate take place? Who is on each side? What arguments are put forward by the different participants?
- The monks repeatedly argue about laughter and its origins. What theories and arguments are advanced by each side? What role do these arguments play in the story?
- The novel features many lists. Identify some of them. What is their purpose? What effect is the author aiming for?
- The novel is divided into days and times of prayer. What effect does this division have?
- "[N]ot all truths are for all ears" (p. 29). What is this quotation referring to? According to the different characters, should knowledge be

censored or not? What do you think?
- In the story, William says: "Often books speak of other books" (p. 277). Comment on this sentence with regard to the novel as whole.
- "Bacon was right: the scholar's first duty is to learn languages!" (p. 354). Explain in what ways language plays a crucial role in the story.
- What are the different characters' opinions about heresy? Does Eco try to remain neutral, or does he try to influence his readers?
- After a conversation with Ubertino, William says: "I have the impression that hell is heaven seen from the other side" (p. 58). What does this mean in the context of the novel?

*We want to hear from you!
Leave a comment on your online library
and share your favourite books on social media!*

FURTHER READING

REFERENCE EDITION

- Eco, U. (2004) *The Name of the Rose.* London: Vintage.

ADAPTATION

- *The Name of the Rose.* (1986) [Film]. Jean-Jacques Annaud. Dir. Italy: Neue Constantin Film.

Bright
≡Summaries.com

More guides to rediscover your love of literature

Animal Farm BY GEORGE ORWELL

The Stranger BY ALBERT CAMUS

Harry Potter and the Sorcerer's Stone BY J.K. ROWLING

The Silence of the Sea BY VERCORS

Antigone BY JEAN ANOUILH

The Flowers of Evil BY BAUDELAIRE

www.brightsummaries.com

Although the editor makes every effort to verify the accuracy of the information published, BrightSummaries.com accepts no responsibility for the content of this book.

© BrightSummaries.com, 2018. All rights reserved.

www.brightsummaries.com

Ebook EAN: 9782806273543

Paperback EAN: 9782806273550

Legal Deposit: D/2015/12603/601

This guide was written with the collaboration of Claire Mathot and translated with the collaboration of Rebecca Neal for the character studies of Adso of Melk, William of Baskerville and Jorge of Burgos, and for the sections "A hybrid novel", "The role of religion", "Intertextuality" and "The symbol of the labyrinth".

Cover: © Primento

Digital conception by Primento, the digital partner of publishers.

Printed in Great Britain
by Amazon